XML
Fast Start

Smart Brain Training Solutions

Thank you for purchasing *XML Fast Start*! We hope you'll look for other *Fast Start* guides from Smart Brain Training Solutions.

Table of Contents

1. Introduction

XML, or eXtensible Markup Language, is a programming language that can be used to describe other languages and a specification for storing information. Although XML and HTML may seem to have a lot in common, in reality the difference between them is like the difference between night and day. HTML is used to format information, but it isn't very useful when it comes to describing information. For example, you can use HTML to format a table, but you can't use HTML to describe the data elements within the table. The reason for this is that you can't really depict something as abstract as a distributor or a customer with HTML, which is where XML comes into the picture. XML can be, and is, used to define the structure of data rather than its format.

What makes XML so powerful is that any type of data—even abstract data concepts—can be given form and structure. You give data concepts—such as distributor, purchase order, and inventory—form by describing their components and the relationship between those components. Instead of the abstract concept of a distributor, you have a specified structure that describes the distributor-related information, such as distributor name, contact name, and address.

You could define the structure of an inventory item handled by the distributor with components such as item number, name, description, unit cost, and suggested retail price.

XML gets this power and versatility from SGML, but it does so without the complexities that make SGML difficult to implement and use on the Web. With this solution, you get the best aspects of SGML without the overhead, which makes XML practical for transmission and use in cyberspace. A key difference between XML and other similar technologies is that XML is used to define the structure of data rather than its format. This means you can use XML to describe the individual data components in a document. For example, using XML you could define the structure of an employee record with components such as employee ID number, full name, contact information, and position within the company. These components could then be further broken down to their basic level.

Although XML can give data structure, you can't use XML to detail how the content is to be rendered. To do this, you have to rely on another technology to format the information. One way to format XML data structures is to combine them with HTML. Here, you create so-called XML islands within standard HTML documents. You use HTML to format the contents of the document, including the data, and you use XML to define the structure of the data. Another formatting solution for XML is to create a style sheet detailing how each piece of the data structure should be formatted. Although a special style sheet language called

Extensible Stylesheet Language (XSL) is designed specifically for this purpose, you could also use the cascading style sheet language.

Generally, XML-only documents end with the .xml extension. You can use this extension to tell the application reading the document that it contains XML data. To interpret the data structures within the document, the application relies on an XML processor. Two general types of XML processors are used: those that validate documents and those that don't. A validating XML processor checks the structure of documents; a nonvalidating XML processor doesn't.

Note In practice, XML-only documents created for Web browser display should end with the .xml extension. If you're developing for a different environment, the extension doesn't really matter. The XML parser classes that you use to interpret the document don't need the extension. However, for consistency, it's best to use the .xml extension for files that contain XML. This ensures that other developers (including yourself at a later date) know what the files contain.

Most XML processors are implemented as extension modules for existing applications. In this context, the XML processor is used within the application to extract information from the XML document and display it in an application window. This window could be in your Web browser or in a stand-alone application.

XML processors are also implemented in programming languages like Java and C#. Here, you use the processor classes to help you extract information from an XML document and display it in an application or applet window.

> **Tip** Another name for a processor is a parser. Not only are there XML parsers, but there are XSL parsers as well. XSL parsers are used to process style sheet definitions in XML documents and render the documents according to those definitions.

2. Using XML

Using XML is a lot easier than you might think. That's because with XML you're in control. Unlike HTML, XML doesn't rely on predefined tags and attributes. This allows you to structure the data in an XML document anyway you like. You define the tags for components within the document. You add attributes to these tags as necessary, and you decide how the components fit together.

The general set of rules for a document's tags and attributes is defined in a document type definition (DTD). XML processors can use the DTD to determine if the document is constructed properly and the processor can pass this information along to the application rendering the document. Keep in mind that documents don't have to have DTDs. However, if they do have a DTD, they should be structured to conform to the DTD.

Once the DTD for a particular type of data is created, you can use the DTD either by inserting it directly into the document, or by referencing the DTD so that it can be imported into the document by the XML processor. Next, you need to create the body of the XML document. There are several ways to do this, and the method you choose depends primarily on how the data is used.

If you're working with fixed data records that change infrequently, you may want to create the necessary data structures using an authoring tool. Here, you insert the data directly into a document and save the result to a file so that it can be viewed directly in an application or compatible browser. You could then publish the document on the Web where others could access it. When you need to update the document, you'd load the document into the authoring tool's editor, make the necessary changes, and then publish the updated document.

If you're working with data that changes frequently, you probably need a more dynamic solution, and rather than creating static documents you could create documents on the fly. To do this, you'd use a document publishing or content management system. These systems are usually integrated with a database. The database stores data records so they can be retrieved on demand. The management system reads in the data and converts it to the appropriate structure based on the DTD and then passes this data off to an application or browser for viewing. Users accessing the dynamic document don't know all this is happening in the background, and they can still access the document using a Uniform Resource Locator (URL).

Extensions to XML

As with most Web technologies, the XML specification is only a starting point. The specification describes XML's core functionality, such as how

XML documents are to be defined, and the necessary grammar that enables documents to comply with this definition.

Beyond the core language, several extensions have been defined, including XML Linking Language, XML Pointer Language, Extensible Stylesheet Language (XSL), XML Namespaces, and XML Schema. These technologies are direct extensions of XML that are defined in XML.

Another technology that you'll learn about in this book is XPath. XPath isn't defined in XML—that is, it's a non-XML language. It is, however, a useful technology that is used with XML.

XLink and XPointer

The XML Linking Language (XLink) and the XML Pointer Language (XPointer) are related. XLink defines the relationship between objects—think hypertext reference. XPointer details how to reference specific structures within a document—think internal links within pages. Together, you can use these technologies to create hypertext links for XML documents.

Unlike the simple unidirectional links defined in HTML, XML links are much more sophisticated. Because XML links can be multidirectional, a single XML link can point to multiple resources and you can move through these resources in any order. For example, in an index, a link could point to all references to the word "hypertext" and you could access these resources in any order and then go back to the index using the single link. XML links are also *self-describing*, meaning a link can contain text that describes the resources it relates to.

XSL

XSL provides rich formatting for XML documents. Using XSL, you can define rules that specify how to extract information from an XML document and how to format this information so that it can be viewed. Often, XML data is transformed into another format, such as HTML—as is the case for Microsoft's XSL processor. Because XSL uses XML as its syntax, you don't need to learn yet another markup language.

> **Note** Applications that extract information from XML documents need an XML parser. Applications that extract information from documents and display their contents using XSL style sheets need an XML parser and an XSL parser. While many Web browsers, including Microsoft Internet Explorer, have a built-in XML and XSL parser, applications written in Java or C# must use XML and XSL parser classes to handle the extraction and presentation tasks.

XML Namespaces

XML Namespaces provide easy access to document structures and prevent namespace conflicts within documents that may use like-named structures. By giving each structure a universal name, a document can use markup defined in multiple namespaces, which is pretty cool when you think about it.

XML Schema

With XML Schema, you can create schemas that describe the characteristics of data structures within documents. For example, in the schema you can define how structures are used, how they're grouped together, and how different structures are related. If you're familiar with XML DTDs, you might be thinking that schemas sound a lot like DTDs—and you'd be right. Schemas provide the same functionality as DTDs. However, because XML schemas are written in XML, they're easy to use and completely extensible, making them much more powerful than DTDs.

XPath

XPath is a non-XML language used to identify specific parts of XML documents. Using XPath, you can write expressions that refer to specific structures in a document. These expressions can be used to match and select elements in an input document and copy it into an output document or to process the elements further. XPointer uses the concept of using XPath to identify specific parts of a document to identify the location to which an XLink links. XPath also supports simple arithmetic, string manipulation, and Boolean expressions.

Creating XML-Based Solutions

To create effective XML solutions, developers need many tools. The key tools they may want to use include authoring tools, application development environments, and database and data integration solutions.

Authoring Tools

Creating XML documents isn't easy. Before you get started, you need to decide how to structure data within documents, and, unfortunately, each project typically is different. The reason for this is that the way you might structure inventory data is very different from the way you might structure customer account data. To make matters worse, you may need to define the data structures in a DTD, and DTDs aren't exactly user-friendly.

Enter XML authoring tools, the easy way to define data structures and create documents using those structures. Most XML authoring tools on the market are actually integrated XML/SGML authoring tools. The reason for this is that XML is a subset of SGML and it's very logical to extend existing SGML tools so they're compatible with XML.

Application Development Environments

Application development environments provide a toolkit that can help you implement XML solutions. Because most of these toolkits come complete with XML parsers, conversion utilities, and more, you can be sure that you'll be able to start and finish an XML-based project.

Database and Data Integration Solutions

Databases can use XML to structure information extracted from the database so that it can be distributed and published. Data integration solutions take this concept a few steps further by using XML to automate the exchange of data. Generally speaking, with an integration solution XML serves as an interface layer or wrapper for data being passed between data sources. This makes it possible for a wide variety of applications, legacy systems, and databases to exchange information.

XML Document Structure

XML documents, like Hypertext Markup Language (HTML) documents, contain text and can be written using any text editor or word processor, such as Microsoft Notepad. For ease of reference, XML documents normally are saved with the .xml extension. The .xml extension ensures that the document is easily recognized as containing XML and that applications, such as Microsoft Internet Explorer, view the document as such.

XML documents are built using text content marked up with tags. For a document describing items in an inventory, these tags could be <item>, <item_number>, <item_name>, and <item_description>. In addition to tags, XML documents can contain other types of markup, including attributes, processing instructions, entity references, comments, and character data. Each of these types of markup is discussed in this chapter.

XML Naming Rules

XML uses the same building blocks as HTML. Because of this, XML documents can contain elements, attributes, and values. Elements are the most basic parts of XML documents. They can contain other elements and text.

The names of elements, attributes, and other structures in XML must conform to a specific naming convention. They may include alphanumeric characters, which include the letters a-z and A-Z as well as the numerals 0-9, in addition to non-English letters, numbers, and ideograms, such as α, β, χ, and δ. They may also include three punctuation characters:

☐ Underscore (_)

☐ Hyphen (-)

☐ Period (.)

> **Note** The only other punctuation character allowed in the names for XML structures is colon (:). The colon character is reserved for XML namespaces.

Names for XML structures may not contain white space, and they may not begin with a hyphen, a period or a number. They may, however,

begin with the English letters A to Z, ideograms, and the underscore
character. This means that while the following are invalid element
names:

```
<.inventory></.inventory>
< item26></ item26>
<product^inventory></product^inventory>
```

The following are valid names:

```
<_inventory></_inventory>
<item26></item26>
<product-inventory></product-inventory>
```

3. Working with Root, Parent, and Child Elements

XML documents are processed a bit differently than other types of documents. With XML, documents should be structured as a tree that processors can navigate easily using method or function calls. Because of this, every XML document has a root element, which is the basis or starting point of the tree hierarchy.

Understanding Root Elements

The root element is the first element in a document, and it contains all other elements. In the following example, inventory is the root element and all other elements are contained within it:

```
<inventory>
    <item tracking_number="459323" manufacturer="Not
listed">
        <item_type>Oak Nightstand</item_type>
        <description>Single-drawer nightstand. Solid
oak.</description>
    </item>
    <item tracking_number="459789" manufacturer="Not
listed">
        <item_type>Oak Desk</item_type>
        <description>Writer's desk with large drawer.
Solid oak.</description>
    </item>
</inventory>
```

Every well-formed XML document has one, and only one, root element. In the example, the inventory element is the parent of the item elements. That is, the inventory element contains the item elements. Every element, except the root element, has exactly one parent element.

Understanding Parent and Child Elements

Parent elements, such as the item elements in the previous example, can contain other elements. These elements are called child elements. In the previous example, the child elements of item are item_type and description. Tags at the same level in a tree hierarchy, such as item_type and description, are referred to as siblings.

Nesting Parent and Child Elements

In XML you can't overlap tags. The opening and ending tags of child elements must be inside the parent element and can't overlap with the tags of siblings.

The following code is improperly formatted:

```
<item>
   <item_type><description>Oak Nightstand
   </item_type></description>
</item>
```

To properly format the example, the item_type and description elements can't overlap. This means the code should be written as:

```
<item>
   <item_type>Oak Nightstand</item_type>
   <description></description>
</item>
```

Adding Root Elements to Documents

To add a root element to a document, follow these steps:

1. Open an XML document for editing, or create a new document.

2. At the beginning of the document, type **<name>**, where *name* is the name of the element that will contain the rest of the elements in the document. The name must conform to the XML naming rules discussed in the previous section.

3. Enter other structures as necessary (using the techniques discussed later in this chapter).

4. Type **</name>**, ensuring that *name* exactly matches the name used in Step 2.

Note While no other elements are allowed outside the root element, other XML structures, such as processing instructions and schemas, can be placed before the start of the root element. You'll find a discussion of processing instructions later in this text.

4. Defining XML Elements and Tags

XML has no predefined elements. You can create any elements you like in XML documents. In most cases you use element names that identify the content and make it easier to process the information later. XML elements are written in one of two forms; either with beginning and ending tags, or as empty tags. Each form can have a special meaning.

The sections that follow examine the key element types and how elements are used in XML documents.

Using Elements with Beginning and Ending Tags

All elements have an opening tag and an ending tag. In the opening tag, the element name is written between less than (<) and greater than (>) signs, such as <item>. In the ending tag, the element name is written between a less than symbol followed by a slash (</) and a greater than (>) sign. For example, inventory item could have an opening tag of <item> and an ending tag of </item>.

> **Note** XML is used to define data structures and not formatting. With this in mind, it's important to remember that the names of XML elements reflect the type of content inside the element and not how that content will be formatted on the screen.

Everything between an element's opening tag and its ending tag is the element's content. In a document the item element could be used as follows:

```
<item>Oak Nightstand</item>
```

Here, the element's content is the text string:

```
Oak Nightstand
```

Although any white space between the opening and ending tag is part of the content, most applications, including Web browsers, choose to ignore it. This means the element content's could be entered into the document as:

```
<item>
Oak Nightstand
</item>
```

or even:

```
<item>
       Oak Nightstand
</item>
```

and it'll be handled the same way. In the example, <item> and </item> are markup and the text string Oak Nightstand—and any white space around it—is character data.

The only characters you can't use in content are the less than symbol (<) and the ampersand symbol (&). These characters are reserved by XML and must not be used as part of the normal text in a document. Instead of using the < or & symbol, you must use an escaped value called a *predefined entity reference*. When an XML parse sees this escape value, it replaces the value with the actual character. (For more information, see the section of this chapter entitled "Using Predefined Entity References.")

Unlike HTML, XML is case-sensitive. This means that you must enter elements in the same case throughout a document or set of documents and that the case must match the one used in a document's document type definition (DTD)—if one is provided. For example, if you defined an element called employee, the matching tags are <employee> and </employee>. The opening tags <Employee> and <EMPLOYEE> would refer to different elements, as would the ending tags </Employee> and </EMPLOYEE>.

Tip Although you can't start a tag using one case, such as <employee>, and end with a different case, such as </Employee>, you can use lower, upper, or mixed cases in element names. The key is that the case must be consistent within any one element.

To add an element with beginning and ending tags to a document, follow these steps:

1. Open an XML document for editing. If the document doesn't have a root element, add one following the steps outlined in the section of this chapter entitled "Working with Root, Parent, and Child Elements." Afterward, move the insertion point after the opening tag for the root element, making sure to follow the nesting rules as appropriate.

2. Type the opening tag for the element you want to specify, such as <item>. Be sure to follow the naming rules defined in the section of this chapter entitled "XML Naming Rules."

3. Enter any content after the opening tag, such as descriptive text. Afterward, enter the ending tag for the element, such as </item>. The name must match exactly the name used previously.

Using Empty Elements

Not all elements have content. In XML you can define an element without content as an *empty element*. Unlike other elements that have an opening and ending tag, empty elements only have a opening tag, which is specially formatted to indicate that no ending element follows.

Empty elements begin with the less than symbol (<) and end with a slash followed by a greater than symbol (/>). For example, you could write a symbol element as <symbol />. Writing <symbol /> is the same as writing <symbol></symbol>.

In XML you can, in fact, use either technique to write empty elements. You can't, however, write only an opening or ending tag. Doing so would result in the document being improperly structured.

Empty elements can be created as top-level elements just below the root element in the tree hierarchy or as child elements of existing elements. As with other types of elements, empty elements must be properly nested. This means that you could use:

```
<employee>
    <name first="Ted" initial="H" last="Green" />
    <id empnum="123" />
</employee>
```

or

```
<employee>
    <name first="Ted" initial="H" last="Green"></name>
    <id empnum="123"></id>
</employee>
```

However, you could not use:

```
<employee>
    <name first="Ted" initial="H" last="Green">
    </id empnum="123">
</employee>
```

or

```
<employee>
    <name first="Ted" initial="H" last="Green">
    <id empnum="123">
</employee>
</name></id>
```

To add an empty element with a single tag to a document, follow these steps:

1. Open an XML document for editing and then move the insertion point to where you want to insert the empty element. Be sure to follow the proper nesting rules.

2. Type the element you want to specify using the form <name />, such as <item />. Be sure to follow the naming rules defined in the section of this chapter entitled "XML Naming Rules."

To add an empty element with separate opening and ending tags to a document, follow these steps:

1. Open an XML document for editing and then move the insertion point to where you want to insert the empty element. Be sure to follow the proper nesting rules.

2. Type the opening tag for the element you want to specify, such as <item>.

3. Immediately after the opening tag, enter the ending tag for the element, such as </item>.

5. Using XML Attributes

As with elements, attributes are an important part of XML documents. You use attributes to describe characteristics of the data structure you're building.

Defining Attributes

Attributes, which can be contained within an element's opening tag, have quotation-mark delimited values that further describe the data structure that the element represents. For example, the item element could have an attribute called tracking_number, which serves as a tracking number for each item in the inventory. If the tracking number for an Oak Nightstand were 459323, then you could write the item element with the attribute as:

```
<item tracking_number="459323">
Oak Nightstand
</item>
```

> **Note** The equals sign is being used to assign the value to the attribute. The value assigned to the attribute can have white space around the equals sign. Here, the white space would be added purely to make the value easier to read when viewed in a text editor.

Because either single quotation marks or double quotation marks are acceptable, the element could also be written as:

```
<item tracking_number='459323'>
Oak Nightstand
</item>
```

> **Tip** Switching between single quotation marks and double quotation marks is required when the attribute value itself contains either single or double quotation marks. If an attribute value contained single quotation marks, you could use double quotation marks to enclose it. If an attribute value contained double quotation marks, you could use single quotation marks to enclose it.

As shown in the previous examples, attribute values are defined using text strings enclosed by quotation marks. As with element content, attribute values may not use the less than symbol (<) or the ampersand (&). Instead, you should replace these values with the appropriate predefined entity reference. Predefined entity references are also provided for single and double quotation marks to eliminate any confusion that may be caused by having quotation marks inside attribute values.

Elements can have multiple attributes, provided that each attribute has a unique name. If you need to specify an attribute several times, you'll need to create separate elements. For example, you'd write:

```
<employee>
   <name first="Ted" initial="H" last="Green" />
   <job role="contractor" />
   <job role="sales" />
</employee>
```

instead of:

```
<employee>
   <name first="Ted" initial="H" last="Green" />
   <job role="contractor" role="sales" />
</employee>
```

When To Use Attributes

Because both elements and attributes can be used to hold information, you may be wondering which to use when. For example, it's better to write:

```
<item>
   <item_type>Oak Nightstand</item_type>
   <tracking_number>459323</tracking_number>
   <manufacturer>Not listed</manufacturer>
   <description>
    Single-drawer nightstand. Solid oak.
    </description>
</item>
```

or

```
<item tracking_number="459323" manufacturer="Not
listed">
   <item_type>Oak Nightstand</item_type>
   <description>
    Single-drawer nightstand. Solid oak.
    </description>
</item>
```

Unfortunately, there's no clear answer, and different people would have different arguments as to which is correct. Officially, attributes are name-value pairs used with elements (that can contain information about the data or contain actual data). Still, there are some who argue that information contained in attributes is metadata, meaning it's only information about the data rather than being data itself. In the school of thought where attribute values are metadata, you could have attributes, such as lang, used to describe the language used for the element's content, but you wouldn't have attributes that contained actual values, such as an item's description or type.

As you set out to use attributes in XML, you'll probably find that it's better to think of attribute values as both metadata and data. In this way you can use an attribute in a way that makes sense for a specific situation rather than being tied to one school of thought.

You'll often find that the application you're using to display the data will help determine how attributes are used. In some cases applications may be able to process attribute values more easily than they can process the raw contents of elements. In other cases you may want to hide certain types of information from viewers until they perform a specific action that causes the values to be displayed or processed.

Adding Attributes to Elements

Attributes specify additional information for data structures. Elements can have zero or more attributes. The order of attributes doesn't matter as long as the attributes are entered before the closing > of the opening tag.

To add an attribute to an element, follow these steps:

1. After the name of the element in the opening tag and before the closing >, type **attribute=** where *attribute* is the name of the attribute you're adding to the tag. Each attribute name for a given element must be unique. If the element already has an attribute of the same name, the name used for the new attribute must be different.

2. Specify the value for the attribute using either single or double quotation marks, such as "value" or 'value'.

> **Note** Either form of quotation marks is acceptable, as long as the same type of quotation mark is used at the beginning and ending of the value. If the value contains a double quotation mark, however, you should enclose the value in single quotation marks. Similarly, if the value contains a single quotation mark, you should enclose the value in double quotation marks.

6. Working with Entity References, Character Data, Comments, and Processing Instructions

In addition to defining elements, attributes, and values, XML documents can contain entity references, character data sections, comments, and processing instructions. These structures are examined in the sections that follow.

Using Predefined Entity References

Entity references are placeholders for other values or other types of content. XML predefines several entity references that allow you to enter text containing characters that are otherwise reserved in the language or that may be misinterpreted.

The two reserved characters in the language are the less than symbol (<) and the ampersand symbol (&). Characters that can easily be misinterpreted are the greater than symbol (>), the single quotation mark ('), and the double quotation mark ("). This means there are five predefined entity references:

- **<** The less than symbol; reserved for the opening bracket of elements.

- **>** The greater than symbol; normally used for the closing bracket of elements.

- **&** The ampersand symbol; reserved to specify the beginning of an entity reference.

- **"** The straight, double quotation mark; normally used to enclose attribute values.

- **'** The apostrophe or straight single quotation mark; normally used to enclose attribute values.

> **Note**   is not a predefined entity for XML. However, this entity frequently is used in HTML to force whitespace characters. To use this character in XML without resulting in an error, you have to use the actual character code, such as ** **, or define the   entity yourself in the DTD. You'll find detailed information on defining and using encoded characters in the section of Chapter 6 entitled "Using Encoded Characters".

You can use the predefined entity references as part of an elements content, as shown here:

```
<business>J. Henry &amp; Associates</business>
```

With attributes, you can use predefined entity references, as shown here:

```
<business name="J. Henry &amp;
Associates"></business>
```

Entity references, such as " and ', are considered to be markup. When an application processes an XML document containing these references, it replaces the entity reference with the actual character to which it refers. This means that in both cases, J. Henry & Associates is replaced with Green & Associates when it's displayed.

To add an entity reference to a document, follow these steps:

1. Open an XML document for editing and then locate the text that contains a value you need to replace with an entity reference or move the pointer to the position where the value should be inserted.

2. Delete the character you're replacing (if any) and then type the entity reference you want to use, such as &.

Using Character Data Sections

Character data sections allow you to specify areas within an XML document that contain raw character data and aren't to be processed by XML parsers. You'll find that character data sections are useful when you want to include XML, HTML, or other examples containing markup in a document without replacing all the reserved or possibly misinterpreted values with entity references. You can, for example, insert an entire snippet of markup within a character data section.

Character data sections have beginning and ending designators. The beginning designator is <![CDATA[and the ending designator is]]>. Everything within these designators is handled as raw character data and isn't processed. This means the & and < characters can appear within the character data section and they won't be interpreted as markup. The only value that can't appear within a character data section is the end designator]]>.

Here's an example of a character data section in an XML document:

```
<book title="101 Great Golf Destinations">
   <chapter number="3" title="Seaside Golf Resorts">
      <page>
         <![CDATA[ <p> A text paragraph </p>
                   <br /> for line breaks
                   <hr /> for horizontal rules
         ]]>
      </page>
      <main_text></main_text>
   </chapter>
</book>
```

Character data sections can appear anywhere in a document, as long as they're between the opening and ending tags for the root element. To add a character data section to an XML document, follow these steps:

1. Open an XML document for editing and then move the pointer to the position where the character data section should be inserted.

2. Type **<![CDATA[**.

3. Enter the text containing markup or other structures that you want to display but don't want to be parsed.

4. Type **]]>**.

> **Note** The only use for the]]> designator is to end the character data section. Although this prevents you from nesting character data sections within other character data sections, you can insert multiple character data sections into a single document. To do this, you must start and end one section before beginning another section.

Using Comments

Comments are useful in any programming or markup language, and XML is no exception. You can use comments to annotate sections of an XML document or to add general notes for the XML document overall. As with HTML, XML comments begin with <!-- and with -->. Here's an example:

```
<!-- Still working to get the example structures in
correct sequence -->
```

No spaces are required between the double hyphens and the comment

text. This allows you to write:

```
<!--Still working to get the example structures in
correct sequence-->
```

The double hyphen can't appear anywhere else within the comment

text. This prevents you from writing:

```
<!-- Still working -- example structures aren't in
correct sequence -->
```

and

```
<!-- Still working on example structures --->
```

Comments are best used to specify information that may be useful to

other document authors as they set out to work with a document.

Comments aren't displayed in applications, such as Internet Explorer, by

default but can be viewed if the document's source code is available.

However, a document's parsed contents may or may not contain the

hidden comments. The reason for this is that XML parsers may choose

to ignore the comments and not pass them along with the document's

contents.

> **Note** You shouldn't rely on comments being available in an
> application. If you need to pass on information in a document,
> you may want to use processing instructions. Processing
> instructions provide special instructions or additional
> information to the application rendering a document.

Because comments aren't parsed, they can occur anywhere in the text of a document. This means they could occur before the opening root tag or after the ending root tag as well. To add a comment to a document, follow these steps:

1. Open an XML document for editing and then move the pointer to the position where the comment should be inserted.

2. Type <!--.

3. Enter the text for the comment.

4. Type -->.

Using Processing Instructions

Processing instructions are used to pass information to applications. The application processing the document can use the instructions to perform special tasks or simply as a source of additional information regarding a document.

Processing instructions begin with <? and end with ?>. The most commonly used processing instructions are those that specify a style sheet attached to a document and those that set the XML version, encoding, and mode for a document. An example instruction that sets a style sheet is:

```
<?xml-stylesheet href="corp.css" type="text/css"?>
```

An example of a processing instruction that sets version, encoding, and mode follows:

```
<?xml version="1.1" encoding="US-ASCII"
standalone="yes"?>
```

Documents don't have to have either type of processing instruction. However, if they do, certain rules apply:

☐ If a document has a processing instruction that specifies a style sheet, the style sheet is used to format elements in the document. When multiple style sheets are used, the style sheet definitions applied last take precedence over those applied earlier. If you don't declare style definitions for every element in the document, the default font settings are applied.

☐ If a document has a processing instruction that declares the XML version, encoding, and mode, the instruction must be the first line of the document. It can't be preceded by comments, white space, or other processing instructions. (For more information on this type of instruction, see the following section, "Specifying XML Declarations.")

To add a processing instruction to a document, follow these steps:

1. Open an XML document for editing and then move the pointer to the position where the processing instruction should be inserted.

2. Type **<?**.

3. Type the instruction name immediately after the open instruction tag, such as **<?xml** or **<?xml-stylesheet**. Don't use a space between the instruction name and the start of the tag.

4. Enter the body of the instruction.

5. Type **?>**.

7. Specifying XML Declarations

An XML declaration is a processing instruction that sets the version, encoding, and mode for an XML document. Declarations aren't required in documents. However, as stated previously, if they're present, they must be the first line of the document and they must not be preceded by comments, white space, or other processing instructions.

XML declarations can specify three attributes: version, encoding, and standalone, as shown in the following example:

```
<?xml version="1.1" encoding="ISO-8859_1" standalone="yes"?>
```

These attributes have special meaning and are discussed in the sections that follow.

Using the Version Attribute

The version attribute in an XML declaration sets the version of XML used in the document. The current version of XML is 1.1.

If you use an XML declaration, the version attribute is mandatory. The other attributes, however, are optional. Because of this, the following XML declaration is valid:

```
<?xml version="1.1"?>
```

Using the Encoding Attribute

XML parsers assume documents are encoded using either UTF-8 or UTF-16. UTF is the Unicode Transformation Format. Because UTF-8 allows variable length characters, parsers use the first few characters in a document to deduce the number of bytes used to express characters. If necessary, you can set the document encoding using the optional encoding attribute for an XML declaration. In the following example the encoding is ISO-8859 Latin 1:

```
<?xml version="1.1" encoding="ISO-8859_1"?>
```
If a document is written in UTF-8 or UTF-16, the document encoding can be omitted. When any other encoding is specified, the parser reading the document translates characters from the document's native encoding (as set in the encoding attribute of the XML declaration) into Unicode.

UTF-8 and UTF-16 are implementations of the international standard character set, Unicode. XML parsers are required to support both the UTF-8 and UTF-16 implementations of Unicode. Support for other character encoding is optional. Nevertheless, the recommended set of supported encoding includes:

EUC-JP	ISO-8859-4
ISO-10646-UCS-2	ISO-8859-5

ISO-10646-UCS-4	ISO-8859-6
ISO-2022-JP	ISO-8859-7
ISO-8859-1	ISO-8859-8
ISO-8859-2	ISO-8859-9
ISO-8859-3	

Using the Standalone Attribute

The standalone attribute in an XML declaration sets the mode for the document and is optional. You can use two values:

☐ **standalone="no"** If standalone is set to *no*, the document may have to read an external DTD to determine the validity of the document's structures and to determine values for parts of the document that use entities or other references defined in the DTD.

☐ **standalone="yes"** If standalone is set to *yes*, the document doesn't rely on an external DTD. This doesn't mean the document doesn't have a DTD. The document and may have an internally specified DTD. (For more information on DTDs, see Part II "DTDs and Namespaces").

When the standalone attribute isn't set in the XML declaration, the value standalone="no" is assumed. This allows the parser to retrieve a DTD if one is referenced.

8. Creating Well-Formed Documents

Regardless of whether XML documents have a DTD, they must be well-formed. If a document is well-formed, it can be said that the document conforms to specific rules of the XML 1.1 specification, including these rules:

☐ A document must have exactly one root element.

☐ Every start tag must have a matching end tag (or use the empty element format).

☐ Elements can't be nested improperly so that they overlap.

☐ Attribute values must be enclosed within single or double quotation marks.

☐ Attribute names within elements must be unique; elements can't have two attributes with the same name.

☐ Unescaped < and & signs can't appear as part of an element's content or as part of an attribute's value.

☐ Comments and processing instructions can't appear inside tags.

Although the list isn't exhaustive, you can see that there are many rules that determine whether a document is well-formed. The most basic well-formed document is one that contains a single element, such as:

```
<inventory>
   100 Oak Nightstands
</inventory>
```

This basic document can be read and understood by XML parsers. It meets all the constraints of the previous rules. However, most documents you'll work with will be considerably more complex and it'll be much more difficult to determine if the document is well-formed. In fact, if you create an XML document by hand, you can almost be assured that it'll contain some type of well-formedness error.

One way to determine if a document is well-formed is to load the document into a Web browser that includes an XML parser, such as Internet Explorer. If there are problems with the document, the browser should display an error message. As you correct each error, additional errors may be displayed when you reload the document.

When the document is finally free of errors, the document should load into the browser and display using the default style sheet. Of course, using Internet Explorer to check documents isn't the most sophisticated technique you can use. If you are a programmer, you can use the parser classes from an application programming interface (API), such as Java or C#.

Exchange Online

Fast
Start

A Quick Start Guide for Exchange Online,
Office 365 and Windows Azure!

Smart Brain
Training Solutions